Mental Health Care, What A Zoo!

Published by ZooTREK Enterprises, Incorporated
11085 Little Patuxent Parkway, Suite 208
Columbia, Maryland 21044
Phone: 800-636-8735 Fax: 410-997-4692
e-mail: info@zootrek.com

ISBN: 0-9769626-0-8

Printed in The United States of America

For information pertaining to use of copyrighted material, bulk purchases or distribution rights please contact ZooTREK Enterprises Inc. at the address, phone, fax number or e-mail listed above.

Page Design: evolve creative graphic design

Printed in the United States of America

First Printing July 2005

ACKNOWLEDGEMENTS AND THANKS

I am grateful to the many people who helped me in this effort. I want to express my special appreciation to Sharon and Ted Major, valued friends of many years, for their interest, encouragement and support. Thanks to my wife Helene for her patient understanding not only during this project but also throughout the time that I have been pursuing a second career as a photographer of zoo animals. For this book she provided creative ideas, helpful thoughts and careful editing. She also accomplished dozens of other tasks that were necessary to prepare the book for publication.

I could not have produced this book without having met and worked with many people who helped me develop my interest in and knowledge about zoos. Posthumous thanks to Dr. Roger Conant, my friend and zoo mentor for 56 years. Thanks to Daniel Moreno, a friend of Roger's and mine for over 55 years, who encouraged me when I first thought of writing about American zoos. He introduced me to the American Zoo and Aquarium Association (AZA). Thanks to all the people in that fine organization and in the zoo field generally who have been so supportive. There are more people in that arena than I can thank with personal acknowledgments, but I want to note my special appreciation to Robert O. Wagner, former Executive Director of the AZA, Sydney Butler, current Executive Director, Kris Vehrs and Robert Ramin (currently with The National Aquarium in Baltimore). You each were helpful in so many ways.

Karen Phillips, my friend and colleague, provided invaluable help in writing this book. She smoothed and refined the rough edges of the text and captions. She has given me encouraging support and has helped greatly by keeping my psychiatric practice and me organized. I could not have developed this book without her assistance.

Thanks to all of you who informally reviewed the drafts and provided critical comments. Thanks to Paul Appelbaum, M.D., Sydney Butler, William Carpenter, M.D., Donald Fandetti, Ph.D., William D.A. Musick, Ph.D., and Steven Sharfstein, M.D. for your gracious pre-publication reviews.

I want to thank everyone who has helped me learn how to be a physician and about psychiatry. You, my formal teachers and supervisors, as well as my patients, have taught me much about what I really needed to know.

And finally, my appreciation to Laura Driskill and Joe Hodanich who provided the graphic design, pre-press and printing services that made this book possible.

TABLE OF CONTENTS

ii. **ACKNOWLEDGEMENTS AND THANKS**

iv. **TABLE OF CONTENTS**

1. Dedication
2. Preface
4. Mental Health Care: General Premise # 1 - Two Heads are Better Than One
6. Mental Health Care: General Premise # 2 - Can We Talk?

9. **THERAPIES**
   - 10. Individual Therapy
   - 12. Couple Therapy
   - 14. Family Therapy # 1
   - 16. Family Therapy # 2
   - 18. Group Therapy
   - 20. Primal Scream Therapy

23. **THERAPISTS**
   - 24. Psychoanalyst
   - 26. Behavior Therapist
   - 28. Psychopharmacologist
   - 30. A Consultant

33. **NORMAL**
   - 34. Normal(?) # 1
   - 36. Normal(?) # 2
   - 38. A Slippery Slope

41. **PERSONALITIES, ILLNESSES AND EXISTENTIAL CONCERNS: NOT QUITE THE DIAGNOSTIC AND STATISTICAL MANUAL (DSM)**
   - 42. Oral Personality
   - 44. Aggressive Personality
   - 46. Narcissistic Personality
   - 48. Paranoid Personality
   - 50. Depression
   - 52. Existential Despair
   - 54. Agoraphobia
   - 56. Narcolepsy
   - 58. Chronic Fatigue Syndrome
   - 60. Excessive Daytime Drowsiness
   - 62. Obesity # 1
   - 64. Obesity # 2
   - 66. Psychophysiologic Headache
   - 68. Social Anxiety Disorder # 1
   - 70. Social Anxiety Disorder # 2
   - 72. General Dissatisfaction Disorder - GDD# 1
   - 74. General Dissatisfaction Disorder - GDD# 2

77. **LOVE**
   - 78. Love # 1 – Early Courtship
   - 80. Love # 2 – The Kiss
   - 82. Love # 3 - Togetherness

85. **PARENTS AND CHILDREN**
   - 86. Mother Love # 1
   - 88. Mother Love # 2
   - 90. Mother Love # 3
   - 92. Mother Love # 4

95. **PLAY AND EXERCISE**
   - 96. Horseplay
   - 98. Physical Fitness # 1
   - 100. Physical Fitness # 2
   - 102. Physical Fitness # 3
   - 104. Physical Fitness # 4

107. **WHAT MAKES US HUMAN?**
   - 108. Inquisitiveness

110. **POSTSCRIPT**

111. **THE END**

112. **ABOUT THE AUTHOR**

DEDICATION

I will always be grateful for the love and support that I received throughout my life from my parents. At times their lives were very difficult but they invariably gave the needs of their children very high priority.

They permitted me freedoms that allowed me to take risks, fail from time to time and grow into the strength of my adult years. They supported my independent spirit, even when it must have been very difficult for them to do so. They encouraged and supported my interests in zoos and in the study of medicine. To them, to their memories, I dedicate this book. I think that they would have enjoyed reading it. Mom, Dad, I love you!

I also dedicate this book to my children Mark, Ellen, Marsha and Steven and to my grandchildren Rebecca, Sarah, Naomi and Noah. You are the future; representatives of life's continuity. I love all of you so very much. May your lives be happy, fulfilling and forces for good in a world of peace.

PREFACE

"This place is a zoo!" I'm certain that you have heard that phrase before. We characterize any place or situation that appears to be busy, wild, chaotic or out of control as a zoo. Real zoos – those accredited by the American Zoo and Aquarium Association, for example, are anything but "a zoo". Dedicated zoo professionals care for their charges with patience and love. Daily life must be well planned, not at all "like a zoo".

Food must be obtained and prepared. Housing must be well designed, clean, temperature-controlled and made safe for both animal residents and their human caretakers. Exhibits must be attractive, educational and maintained in excellent condition – despite the fact that many of the residents might choose to eat their exhibits' vegetation! The staff must attend to the thousand and one other activities necessary to make life comfortable, safe and interesting for the animals, staff and visitors.

However, the expression "What A Zoo!" is well ingrained in our vocabulary and mental images. It seems to me that many aspects of life might be considered "zoo-like", including a few in my own field of psychiatry.

Zoos have always fascinated me; it's not just the animals and plants that I find intriguing, but also the sense of wilderness in the midst of cities and the dedicated men and women who care for their charges as labors of love. I have been visiting zoos regularly since I was eleven years old. At age twelve I was invited to join the Junior Zoological Society of Philadelphia. This group of teenagers met weekly at the zoo where we presented papers to each other about animals and shared our common interests in wildlife. The JZSP, started by Roger Conant, was my introduction into the world of science.

By age thirteen I was working as a volunteer on Saturday afternoons for Dr. Conant, then Curator of Reptiles and later Director of the Philadelphia Zoo. I am pleased and almost amazed to say that he and I remained good friends for more than 56 years until his recent death. This extraordinary, talented and very productive man was a mentor, father figure and, especially in recent years, a person whose friendship I valued highly. Still active and publishing scientific papers at age 92, he was truly an "Iron Man" of herpetologists.

After studying pharmacy at Temple University and medicine at Jefferson Medical College, I entered the specialty of psychiatry. However, I never lost my interest in animals, zoos and the people who work in the field. Visiting zoos had always been my major hobby. In 1988 I began to devote increasing time, energy and resources to this interest. While maintaining my psychiatric practice I started a second career of writing and photo-illustrating zoo-themed materials. Since then I have visited more than 200 zoos in the United States, Canada and Europe, traveling well over 80,000 miles and taking more than 100,000 photographs of animals and zoo scenery.

When I told friends, colleagues and patients that I was visiting "zoos", many thought that the term was a euphemism for visiting psychiatric facilities. I explained to them that I never use such a term when referring to psychiatry and that I was traveling around the country visiting real zoos.

However, the concept of "the psychiatric zoo" intrigued me and prompted me to select photographs with a psychiatric/psychological motif for this book. I hope that you will read it with good humor and I trust that no one will take offense at any of the mental images that may be evoked.

MENTAL HEALTH CARE: GENERAL PREMISE # 1

When problems arise in life and new strategies and approaches may be needed, two heads are better than one!

The only two-headed, eight-legged horse in the world!

MENTAL HEALTH CARE: GENERAL PREMISE # 2

Most psychotherapeutic interventions depend on verbal interactions between patients and therapists.

"Can We Talk?"

THERAPIES

Mental Health therapies abound: Talk therapies, visual imagery therapies, dance therapies, behavior therapies, cognitive therapies, brief therapies, long-term therapies, psychopharmacological therapies, individual, couple, family, group therapies and more, all compete for the interest of patients and therapists alike. How is a person to choose among such a variety of possibilities? How do therapists and patients choose the best fit?

INDIVIDUAL THERAPY

Individual, psychoanalytically oriented psychotherapy has been the basis of many psychotherapeutic interactions for more than a century. Confidentiality, leading to greater openness of communications than might otherwise be possible, is essential so that patients may feel safe while providing more accurate, complete and highly personal information. The female patient in this photograph is able to discuss her frigid feelings during the winter because she knows that her privacy will be respected. During the last half of the twentieth century newer forms of interactive psychotherapies such as group and family therapy, as well as new theoretical formulations about therapy have become part of the mental health armamentarium.

"Now tell me, what do you mean when you say you feel 'frigid'?"

COUPLE THERAPY

Couples may find themselves communicating poorly and struggling to see each other's points of view before marriage, during marriage – or even after a marriage ends. Couple therapy may help strengthen difficult relationships or may help couples separate in a more humane fashion.

"We just don't seem to see eye to eye."

FAMILY THERAPY # 1

Family therapy can be a very effective way of helping family members cope with many problems. These include the complex issues that invariably present themselves when parents and children struggle with establishing rules, roles and identities.

The family therapist tries to help family members talk and behave with each other in a more constructive fashion than they usually do. By providing a neutral territory and being a caring facilitator, the therapist attempts to help family members identify problem areas and develop workable solutions. These difficult areas may include various interpersonal rivalries and struggles, anger management, ways to express love and support and many other issues with which family members struggle.

"It's not often that we have a chance to get together and talk about the way we feel about each other."

FAMILY THERAPY # 2

Sibling rivalries are observed among many animal species. Strengths and weaknesses are tested, sometimes with fatal results for weaker siblings. The struggles seem to play a role in nature's need to produce strong adults. Human siblings also compete with each other – sometimes constructively and sometimes not. Siblings may carry on with such behavior long after childhood. When the competition gets to be too fierce or destructive, family therapy may be of help. (Would it have helped in the difficulties experienced by Cain and Abel or Jacob and Esau?)

"I told you before to get away! You may be my twin brother, but these grubs and berries are mine!"

GROUP THERAPY

Talking with other people who are experiencing similar problems can prove very therapeutic. Patients are best able to share experiences, thoughts, feelings and strategies for coping with life's vicissitudes when in a relatively safe environment.... separate from the jungle of everyday life.

"I feel good meeting with you all each week to discuss our problems."

PRIMAL SCREAM THERAPY

Primal scream therapy is not as popular as it once was. However, giving vigorous vent to inner anger and pain may be very therapeutic. There is still value in a healthy roar or two. Even a therapist may feel the need to "let it out" after a tough day at the office.

"Aarrgh – Mmm, that feels so much better!"

THERAPISTS

Therapists abound: physical therapists, acupuncture therapists, dance therapists, art therapists, and herbal therapists, to name but a few. More types of therapists exist than I can list.

Many people think of psychotherapists when they speak of "Therapists". Even these therapists come in a variety of garbs: Freudian, Neo-Freudian and Non-Freudian analysts, behavior therapists, cognitive therapists, twelve-step therapists and others. In addition to their different educational backgrounds and theoretical or ideological positions, therapists can be male or female, old or young, "strict constructionists" or flexibly eclectic.

Stereotypes run rampant: benevolent, understanding, empathic analysts; coolly emotionless behaviorists; laid-back therapists from California; chic "communication specialists"; spiritual, earth-loving gurus advising "holistic" approaches; and somber, moralizing but all-loving pastoral counselors.

Therapists spend their lives trying to help people in distress. Some people occasionally make them objects of scornful humor. I have attempted to depict a few of the stereotypes in the following pages, but only with good will and respectful humor. The therapists presented in the following pages illustrate some of these stereotypes and bear no resemblance to any persons living or dead (unless you happen to recognize yourself or YOUR therapist).

PSYCHOANALYST

A well-trained psychoanalyst or psychoanalytically oriented psychotherapist knows that there may be many meanings behind a patient's silence, words, phrases or gestures. Such therapists consider what their patients mean by both their overt and covert messages. They attempt to help patients understand the meanings and influences of their subconscious thoughts and feelings; increasing their self-understanding and alleviating to some extent the pain of those distressing thoughts and feelings.

"I wonder what she meant by that?"

BEHAVIOR THERAPIST

Behavior therapists pay great attention to the behaviors that their patients exhibit and to their patients' responses to environmental stimuli. They do not believe that focusing on and interpreting a patient's unconscious thoughts is the preferred method of helping patients overcome self-defeating and distressing thoughts and behaviors. They generally do not refer to themselves as "touchy-feely" therapists.

"Tell me again why you object to my behavior modification therapy?"

PSYCHO-PHARMACOLOGIST

Research psychopharmacologists study the effects of many chemicals on human thoughts, feelings and behaviors. Clinical psychopharmacologists use these compounds to treat a variety of distressing conditions such as anxiety disorders, mood disorders and psychotic disorders, including schizophrenia. Botanist pharmacologists, such as the "man of the forest" shown here examining plants, know that the natural chemical factories found in tropical rain forests and elsewhere produce many chemicals that may some day become useful medicines.

"I wonder whether some of these plants might be of help in treating depression?"

A CONSULTANT

Consultants answer the difficult questions. When a therapist wonders about possible co-existing medical problems, an internist or neurologist may be of help.

When a psychotherapist has a question about a patient's diagnosis, medications or about psychotherapeutic treatment approaches, a well-trained psychiatric or other consultant may be of help.

But be forewarned. Consultants may present a large bill!!

"I have to admit it. This case certainly has me puzzled."

NORMAL

Mental health services generally deal with conditions we describe as illnesses or disorders of personality and behavior. In order to assess and treat the abnormal, we need to understand what are normal thought, mood and behavioral states. This is not easy. Different societies and divisions within societies may have very diverse cultural expectations. One culture may demand that its members be very emotionally expressive with each other and others may demand emotional reserve. One culture may expect flamboyance in dress and another very plain appearance. There are groups of people who are open and friendly and others who are reserved and suspicious. A therapist needs to have a broad knowledge of the differences in normal subgroups of the human species in order to differentiate normal from abnormal behaviors.

NORMAL? #1

Some people appear to be narcissistic or even aggressive.
In reality they may be brimming with self-confidence earned
by successful past endeavors.

"I am NOT narcissistic. I just strut around because I'm cocksure of myself!"

NORMAL? #2

People have different value systems and different personalities. One person may be somewhat shy, introverted and conservative in dress; another more outgoing and flamboyant. Both styles can be within the normal limits of human behavior.

"I don't think that there is anything wrong with dressing well and strutting my stuff, so please stop calling me a turkey."

A SLIPPERY SLOPE

"Normal" human behavior ordinarily means following certain accepted social rules. However, many people are adventurous and from time to time like to challenge the rules. Sometimes such challenges work out well and may even lead to a better society. Civil rights uprisings throughout the world that lead to increased democracy and freedom for oppressed people exemplify such constructive behavior. Sometimes these behaviors may lead down a slippery slope to an undesirable outcome. Traveling down this slippery slope of breaking accepted rules can be dangerous.

"I'm telling you that I'm OK. I won't slip into dangerous behavior."

PERSONALITIES, ILLNESSES AND EXISTENTIAL CONCERNS: NOT QUITE THE DIAGNOSTIC AND STATISTICAL MANUAL (DSM)

We will now explore some of the many problems that bring patients and clients to see therapists. Some of these are personality problems – ingrained, life-long styles of viewing and dealing with the world. Some of these difficulties are classic "psychiatric" illnesses, many of which, within recent years, have been shown to have strong biochemical components. Others deal with the ultimate meaning of the universe and creation and the struggles many of us undergo at some time trying to determine purpose and meaning in our own existence.

ORAL PERSONALITY

Oral satisfactions begin at birth. Our first, and perhaps most lasting pleasures, come from sucking and swallowing. As infants we drink milk from a breast or bottle; as adults we drink milk and other satisfying liquids (soft drinks, beer, wine and liquor), eat foods, chew gum, smoke cigarettes and talk. Although most people enjoy oral pleasures, some people do so much more than others.

"All of my life I have enjoyed good food and drink – and lots of it!"

AGGRESSIVE PERSONALITY

Some people behave meekly and timidly. Others behave very assertively. Those who strive more fiercely than others may not seem to think or care about the feelings and rights of others. They may approach the world in a very aggressive and even "biting" manner.

"I can't understand why so many people are afraid of me. I think I have a wonderful smile!"

NARCISSISTIC PERSONALITY

Self-awareness is an important component of mental and physical health. Too much focus on the self, however, and inadequate attention to the people with whom we live and work, can lead to difficult interactions with others.

"Mirror, mirror on the wall. . . who's the most beautiful bird of all?"

PARANOID PERSONALITY

A little healthy caution is prudent; but sometimes prudence is replaced by paranoia and threats are perceived where none exist. We see this in individuals as well as cultures and nations. They are constantly searching for potential enemies... or feel that they have found them.... or think that they are being watched or otherwise spied upon.

"I can't help thinking that someone is always staring at me."

DEPRESSION

Depression-like moods arise from many causes. We use the term to indicate conditions that differ in significant respects. We say that people are "depressed" when they suffer from unhappiness, grief, existential despair and psychological depression from loss – or the classical concept of "anger turned inward". The term "clinical depression" or "major depression" has now become widely used to indicate a biochemically based depression associated with insufficient availability of certain neurotransmitters.

People suffering from severe, biochemically-based depression often feel hopeless, profoundly sad and guilt-ridden. They are often tearful and functionally immobile. They may sleep for too little or too much time; they may eat very little or eat too much. A crushing weight has descended upon them and most activities seem to be burdensome. Life appears to be bleak and dark.

"The world seems dark and dreary to me. How could things get bleaker?"

EXISTENTIAL DESPAIR

What is the meaning of the universe? How was it created? What is the meaning of life? Or more importantly for most people, "What is the meaning of THEIR life?". To some extent that question is an essential part of being human. The question has philosophical, spiritual and psychological dimensions and is frequently encountered in the therapist's office. Use of the term "depression" may indicate pain about aspects of a person's life such as despair over a colorless existence. More often, despair is associated with more spiritual or philosophical concerns about the meaning of human existence.

"I really feel sad. My life is so colorless and seems to be without meaning."

AGORAPHOBIA

The term originally meant, “Fear of the marketplace”. Indeed, today many people with agoraphobia cannot leave their homes to shop in stores or for any other reason. They virtually become prisoners in their own homes. They may experience sudden episodes of great emotional fear and very unpleasant physiological reactions. We name these conditions “panic states” or “acute anxiety reactions”.

Treatment with a combination of psychotherapy and medication can be very effective in lessening the pain, social isolation and severe disability associated with agoraphobia.

"I get a panic attack whenever I move outside of this log. I'm NOT coming out. I'm NOT coming out!"

NARCOLEPSY

Sufferers from narcolepsy feel awake one moment and, without warning, fall asleep the next. The period of sleep may last just seconds, but they can be important seconds indeed – especially if they occur while the person is driving an automobile. Thankfully, effective treatments are available for this potentially very serious illness.

"I suddenly fall asleep at the most inopportune times."

CHRONIC FATIGUE SYNDROME

Many people complain of great fatigue and lack of energy. They seem unable to function other than at a bare minimum level. The cause is still debated, as is the validity of the concept itself. Some clinicians doubt whether there truly is such a biologically based condition. Others insist that it does exists. The quest for answers goes on.

"I feel tired, weak and down for the count most of the time."

EXCESSIVE DAYTIME DROWSINESS

Excessive daytime drowsiness may be noticed when people have to work double shifts, maintain two jobs, work different time-based shifts or don't obtain sufficient sleep. Such sleepiness must be distinguished from chronic fatigue syndrome and narcolepsy because treatment approaches and recommendations are different in each case.

"I get very tired when I have to work two shifts back to back."

OBESITY #1

Obesity in America is a major health and life-threatening epidemic. Consequences, including heart disease, diabetes and related metabolic illnesses are enormous. Being fat is not funny, despite the many jokes about obese people. Obesity causes grave damage to individuals and produces serious, negative economic consequences for society. Obesity is difficult to treat because of the multiple causative factors, but behavioral interventions can be of significant help.

"Doc, I'm telling you, I eat like a sparrow."

OBESITY #2

Obesity may be caused by emotional problems or cause emotional problems... or both. Treatment often is very difficult and can range from use of behavior modification techniques to gastric stapling and bypass procedures. Calorie control, exercise and a change in life style are vital components of any effective weight loss or weight control system. Support groups provide greatly needed help for any individuals who otherwise might give up their quest for a healthier weight.

"Do you think there's still room for us at the Pachyderms Losing Pounds meeting?"

PSYCHOPHYSIOLOGICAL HEADACHE

Headaches are one of humankind's most common ailments. They may have skeletal and muscular structural, physiological and psychological components. The stressors that we experience in 21st century life certainly haven't helped to reduce our incidence of headaches.

"The tension around here keeps giving me headaches."

SOCIAL ANXIETY DISORDER #1

This condition has existed for a long time but has been recognized and named only recently. Sufferers feel unreasonably shy and become very uncomfortable when they have to interact with other people. Some individuals who suffer from social anxiety appear strong and powerful and, to all outward appearances, should have no need to fear social contacts. Cognitive-behavioral therapy and medication may help to alleviate some of their distress.

"Both of us are really, really shy and don't like going out."

SOCIAL ANXIETY DISORDER #2

Some animals need to be especially shy and reclusive in order to survive! Such a behavioral-emotional pattern may have served as a protective mechanism at one time in human development. In today's world it is generally a significant handicap for most socially phobic people.

"We become very anxious when we have to mix with others. Let's just stay here."

GENERAL DISSATISFACTION DISORDER – GDD # 1

(Not yet in the Diagnostic and Statistical Manual)

I must admit it, I invented this disorder. Some people feel trapped -fenced into their daily lives. A person may feel dissatisfied with his job, income, family life or other elements of his environment. Such dissatisfaction or unhappiness may be mistaken for depression.

The most appropriate treatment for such unhappiness is not necessarily pharmacological; rather it may be an examination of the circumstances of the person's life. Outcomes of such an exploration may be a healthier adaptation to the existing circumstances or may lead to changes in a person's expectations.

"Could my life be better if I left here? Don't fence me in!"

GENERAL DISSATISFACTION DISORDER – GDD # 2

People may describe themselves as depressed, but really mean that they are unhappy and dissatisfied with certain aspects of their lives. They may become envious of what other people have or seem to have. They think that changing their lives in some ways would make them happier. Often, the "greener grass" turns out to be an illusion. Although, the grass CAN occasionally be truly greener on the other side of the fence.

"The grass often seems to be greener on the other side of the fence."

LOVE

Love! What a powerful force in human emotions. The definitions are best left to writers, painters, other artists and philosophers. Love attracts us to each other, gives us strength to raise our children, allows us to live together in friendship, care for one another and, in so many ways, adds to the meaning of our lives. Romantic love, physical love, parental love and love for our friends can contribute to mentally healthy lives.

Sometimes love goes awry and produces pain. Couple therapy may help in bringing the alienated parties back together or helping them to separate in the most humane fashion possible both for their own sake and for the sake of children that they may have. In addition to couple therapy, individual therapy may be of value in helping one or both parties understand how they may have contributed self-defeating behaviors to the relationship.

Patients may learn to become aware of and change disruptive or destructive behaviors in the future; may learn how to deal most effectively with the grief brought about by the unwanted ending of a relationship.

LOVE #1 - EARLY COURTSHIP

Love and romance are in the air. Spring is a special time throughout the animal kingdom. Animals court, pair off or otherwise join together. It has been said that in the spring "a young man's fancy turns to thoughts of love." Romantics say that love is a matter of the heart. As medical scientists, however, we know where the real activity takes place... the brain.

"I love being out here on the water with you, sweetheart. It's such a romantic way to spend an evening."

LOVE # 2 –The Kiss

Ah yes, the warmth of those first kisses; they bring closeness and tenderness. Kissing serves as a powerful bonding experience for most people in love. It may be a brief touch of lips or a deep joining of souls, but kissing brings lovers closer to each other.

"I can't begin to tell you how much I enjoy kissing you, my love."

LOVE #3 - Togetherness

When two compatible people meet and fall in love, they want to spend time together. They search for opportunities to do so. Strolling hand in hand through life, they strengthen their bond. People with happy, loving relationships seem to have much better mental health than people living alone.

"Isn't it wonderful walking through the garden together?"

PARENTS AND CHILDREN

Relationships among parents and children can be among the most satisfying of human experiences. Parents strive to provide a good education for the child while keeping the early bonding experiences alive and healthy. Parents and children need to continue to grow; to move from the early child-parent dependency to one of increasingly healthy independence on the part of the child. Parents often have problems with their offspring. These problems generally are equaled only by the problems that children have with their parents. Communication problems arise. Differences in value systems become evident as children develop their own individual personalities and generational lifestyles. Children struggle for dominance in family units and move inexorably into adulthood. These factors can contribute to the stress in our daily lives as well as to the development of our adaptive strengths. Oh what a job it is for a family to handle those stressors!

(NOTE: See Family Therapy, especially Sibling Rivalry)

MOTHER LOVE # 1

Love often leads to marriage, which in turn, often leads to children. Very few events are as exciting but also as anxiety-producing as having and caring for that first child. Therapists may have to help some parents become good loving parents. Mother-child bonding is critically important, but some mothers may need help managing post-partem depression – a severe condition that can interfere with healthy bonding.

"I love you sweet baby. Drink your breakfast and then we'll swing through the forest for a while."

MOTHER LOVE # 2

The instinctive need for mothers and their children to bond with each other is one of the most powerful drives that mammals experience. Primate mothers, including humans, must teach their young everything they need to know for survival. This includes teaching their youngsters proper nutrition for good physical and mental health.

"Here honey, eat your carrot. It will make you healthy and help you develop good eyesight."

MOTHER LOVE # 3

Parents cannot always fulfill their children's wishes. Some things just have to be the way they are. Humans live in many environments to which their children must adapt for both their physical and mental health. Good parents understand that their child will have a mind of her own. With loving care on the parents' part, adaptation may be easier, and the child will be more likely to grow into a strong, psychologically well-balanced adult. Sometimes Mom and Dad DO know best.

"Mom, couldn't we move to a warmer climate?"

MOTHER LOVE # 4

A psychologically healthy mother will develop a loving relationship with her child. Large cats and small cats are all excellent mothers. They bond closely with their young, protect them and teach them the hunting skills that they will need in order to survive in the wide, wild world. A good human mother will provide warmth, love, acceptance and encouragement to her child to help the child become a comfortable, self-confident adult.

"A Mother's Kiss"

PLAY AND EXERCISE

NOT EVERYTHING RELATING TO MENTAL HEALTH IS COMPLICATED AND SOMBER

As humans we often struggle with powerful emotions of love and anger. Ideally, we also need to know how to relax, have fun and enjoy ourselves. Therefore, if our basic needs are met we play a great deal. Play may be for pure relaxation and pleasure. It can also be used as a mechanism to help strengthen our minds and bodies. Play and relaxation, as well as work, are essential for a well-rounded life and for good mental health.

HORSEPLAY

Everyone needs some time for fun and relaxation. So enjoy reading this book and don't feel guilty thinking that you are "wasting time". Enjoy a little "horsing around" of your own. It will be good for your mental health.

"Wait up, all of you! There's nothing wrong with taking some time for a little horseplay!"

PHYSICAL FITNESS # 1

Encouraging a child to exercise while still young may lead to a lifetime of healthy physical activity. This is good for both physical and emotional health if not overdone – see following page.

"I love playing on this jungle gym."

PHYSICAL FITNESS # 2

Don't overdo things or overreach your abilities. "Sometimes I overestimate my abilities. I thought that I could just jump to the ground from here, but it sure looks like a long way down." Yes, parents sometimes have to help children when they get a bit in over their heads. People with good mental health tend to know their limits and, if they go beyond them and get into trouble, know when to ask for help.

"How did I get myself out on this limb?"

PHYSICAL FITNESS # 3

Adults can keep fit by working out. This gentleman is exercising at his favorite gym. As the child becomes an adult, individual exercise may be the best way to maintain fitness. Joining other people at a gym helps to maintain motivation for the hard work involved. Stretching is an important part of exercising and helps keep people limber as they grow older.

"I like to include stretching exercises when I work out."

PHYSICAL FITNESS # 4

During vigorous exercise we work up a "healthy sweat". It feels good to take a refreshing shower after a workout. Keep in mind that exercise releases endorphins, helps combat depressed moods and tends to relieve the tensions that build up within us.

"I love to take a bath or shower after my workout at the gym."

WHAT MAKES US HUMAN?

Many factors have contributed to the evolution of humans. We have opposable thumbs, we came down from the trees, we walk erect and we have large brains. But one factor above all others has allowed us to take these physical traits and expand our own knowledge. That attribute is inquisitiveness. We explore quarks, the universe and the meaning of our creation. Many animals are inquisitive and investigate their surroundings; but none with the determination, wide-ranging interests and capacities of humans. We humans have expanded our inquisitiveness and spirit of inquiry so that virtually nothing is beyond our wish to explore and understand its nature. We thirst for knowledge. We are the nosiest species on the planet.

INQUISITIVENESS

Many mammals are inquisitive, but the most inquisitive of all are humans. We question everything about ourselves and everything in the universe. Questions And Answers R Us.

"I can't understand why so many people call me nosey. I think that I am just very inquisitive."

POSTSCRIPT

Thank you for taking this tour of mental health care with me. I have tried to present elements of practice from a different perspective than you likely have seen in the past. Obviously we have touched on only a few of the many possible aspects of "mental health care".

Mental health care truly addresses both health and illness. Issues such as love, play and work are important factors in the development and maintenance of good mental health.

I hope that you have enjoyed this exploration. I trust that no one will be offended by any of the representations shown. During the time in which I visited these zoos and took photographs I also maintained an active practice of psychiatry. I believe that my intensive exposure to animal behaviors, albeit viewing captive animals, has enhanced my ability to understand and appreciate the diversity of human behaviors; and has helped me become a better psychiatrist. But that may be wishful thinking and a rationalization. Perhaps all it did was give me a great deal of enjoyment and a bit more knowledge.

That's OK too.

I hope that I have hit the "bull's-eye" with you and that you have enjoyed the book.

Thank you for taking this zoo trek with me.

THE END

ABOUT THE AUTHOR

Carl was born and raised in Philadelphia. He received his B.S. and M.S degrees from Temple University School of Pharmacy and his M.D. from Jefferson Medical College of the Thomas Jefferson University. While serving in the United States Army he completed his Psychiatric Residency at Walter Reed General Hospital and a Post-Residency Fellowship in Community Psychiatry at the Laboratory of Community Psychiatry at Harvard Medical School. After serving as Chief of Mental Health Services at Fort Benning, Georgia and as Chief of the Department of Psychiatry in the Division of Neuropsychiatry at Walter Reed Army Institute of Research, he left the Army as a Lieutenant Colonel in 1971.

Since then, he and his wife Helene have lived in Columbia, Maryland, where they raised their children Mark, Ellen, Marsha and Steven. He served as Director of Howard County's Bureau of Mental Health and Addiction for five years and has had a private practice of psychiatry since 1972. He is a Board Certified Psychiatrist and a Distinguished Life Fellow of the American Psychiatric Association.

He has been interested in visiting zoos since his early childhood. Since 1988 he has visited more than 200 zoos throughout the United States, Canada and Europe. He has observed the evolution of zoos throughout the past three decades. In earlier years, zoos primarily provided recreation and entertainment for their visitors by enclosing animals in cages. Today zoos provide not only recreational and educational opportunities, but have become enormously important facilities that educate people about the need for conservation of our natural habitat resources and the need to preserve the diversity of both animal and plant species. Increasingly, zoos display their animals in naturalistic environments. They have developed research facilities for preservation of our threatened wildlife. The American Zoo and Aquarium Association plays an important role in developing high standards of care for the animals. Accredited zoos periodically undergo rigorous evaluations to be certain that they maintain high quality of their facilities and provide excellent care for their charges.

Carl believes that we can learn a great deal about the essential nature of humanity if we study animal behaviors and social structures more thoroughly than we have in the past . He believes therapists and patients would benefit from more effective application of this knowledge in our theoretical, research and clinical practices. The insights about animal behavior would enhance our understanding of and ability to treat many of the problems we encounter in our day-to-day lives.

He also believes that a good sense of healthy humor is vitally important in attaining reasonable mental health and in providing mental health care services. Laughing WITH, not laughing AT others and ourselves, is essential for us all as we travel the often times difficult trails through the forests of human existence.

Order a little "healthy" humor!

Go to www.zootrek.com to order your copy or

MAIL OR FAX ORDER FORM
ZooTREK Enterprises, Inc.
Suite 208, 11085 Little Patuxent Pkwy.
Columbia, Maryland 21044
FAX NO 410-997-4692

or

Call Customer Service for More Information
PHONE NO 800-636-8735

		QTY	TOTAL
PRICE	$22.95	______	______
SALES TAX 5% *(Maryland Residents Only)*			______
SHIPPING	$5.25 U.S.	______	______
	$10.25 INT'L	______	______
SUBTOTAL			______
TOTAL COST			______

PLEASE PRINT!!

NAME ______________________

STREET ______________________

CITY ______ STATE ______ ZIP ______

PHONE ______________________

PAYMENT OPTIONS

☐ Check or

☐ Credit Card
☐ Visa ☐ MasterCard

NAME OF CARDHOLDER ______________________

CARD NO ______ EXPIRATION DATE (MONTH/YEAR) ______